English Poetry
from Israel

*The Israel Association of Writers in English thanks
The Israel Writers' Federation for their contribution
to the publication of this book.*

Published by the Israel Association of Writers in English,
P.O.B. 39385, Tel Aviv 61393, Israel.

February 1997

Editors: Karen Alkalay-Gut, Lois Ungar and Zygmunt Frankel

Shirley Kaufman's poems *The West is Suffering from Compassion Fatigue* and
For Dear Life are from her collection *Roots in the Air*, reprinted by permission of
Copper Canyon Press, POB 271, Port Townsend, WA 98368, U.S.A.

ISBN 965-222-767-6

Cover by Zygmunt Frankel

CONTENTS:

THE ENGLISH POET IN ISRAEL

Of all the expatriate writers in Israel who persist in writing in a foreign language despite their daily existence in Hebrew, the English ones must be the most independent. They left their various homelands of their own choice, not because of a tragic past, hostile or suppressive government or social persecution, and came here to join in a predominantly Jewish community.

And yet, with deep and conflicting loyalties, at some level they remain foreigners within this community. Some have the common problem of learning a language. Some have never tried to learn Hebrew and exist comfortably among their countrymen in this multi-cultural society. Others speak perfect Hebrew but remain loyal to their mother tongue.

There are writers who perceive their foreignness a handicap, and others who see it as an opportunity for independence and perspective. Even within this small community of writers, there are marked differences. Geography and atmosphere play a part: Jerusalem writers often have different subject matter or moods than Tel Aviv writers, and those in the desert and kibbutzim may have alternative narratives to relate. Background and native culture are additional factors. A poet steeped in American tradition will begin from a different position than another brought up on British literature. But there is one factor which unites them all - an obstinate, sometimes even perverse, affection for the English language.

This book presents a sampling of poets writing in English in Israel. Most are native English speakers, but some have acquired the language and the culture and remain just as loyal to it. The poems were primarily chosen from past issues of "arc", the journal of the Israel Association of Writers in English, devoted to writing by residents of Israel in English.

The Editors

ADA AHARONI

SHOW CANNON AT PLYMOUTH ROCK

We walk around
modest wooden houses
in the New World,
fencing old bearded goats
who have long forgotten
what cannons mean

Sober and smiling pilgrims
in colored bonnets and garters
saunter, peace in the sunshine.
A laced minute-man blows
an ancient cannon,
like a horn, just for show,
and we take snaps and laugh.

The magic feat
breathes unbound hope.
Surely one day all our
cannons will be blown merely for show
and all our guns drawn only by John Wayne
in those old archaic
films of long ago
when blood was merely paint.

KAREN ALKALAY-GUT

I EXPLAIN DARWIN TO THE REBBE

The old man and I sit on the porch -
It is Indian summer and the weather
lures us with our books outside.
And the madness of the season
makes me stop the lesson of Bereisheit
with- -"Rebbe, what do you think of Darwin?"

The rabbi of the "Kippele" shul knows no English- -
we discuss the Bible in Mamme-loshen.
And what has he read
that he should know of "The Origin of Species"
So he asks me to explain - and I do -
in my most grown up eleven year old tone -
about the apes, the jungle, survival
of the fittest.

It is eleven years since the Holocaust.
In the twilight he is silent, rocking
very slightly as he arranges his decision.

"Bobbe Meisses," he says, and I nod,
suddenly in revelation.
"You learn what you must for school
but of course no one can really
believe in such stories."

"ABORTIONS NEVER LET YOU FORGET"
Gwendolyn Brooks

It is true, those unborn babies hang around
the mother that expelled them
much longer than regular children do
tweaking on their dresses and begging
to be bought something, to be fed again,
to be held to be loved.
And sometimes I turn to mine,
gather them up, resigned -
my arms full of their absence.

UNA SELVA

Here
in this dark
sweet forest
I learn
the motions
of the axe -
stretching back
and leaning in
to the timber,
the separate grasp
of two hands
on the helve
sliding together
as the blade
bites the heart,
releasing aroma
of inner wood.

'I'hen the rhythm
of repetition.
It is the most
powerful lesson
of them all -
Over and over
the body eats
even the hardest forest.

SLEEVES

I wake up
and the sleeves of my care
are still raveled, the yarn
wound around my arms
like phylacteries.

This is what it is like
to read Shakespeare and Blake
before sleep in the Holy Land -
the torture of devotion and guilt
as one

RACHEL TZVIA BACK

LETTER FROM THE DESERT

First there were the bones
we buried at crossroads,
mapping our exile, markers
for our return.

Others we lost, and lost then
our way: wandering in our sleep
they rattled, enraged to be
scattered under foreign stones.

But the last bones of promised
last days we carried
like hope across this desert
until we were bent, as in a prayer

we could not pray, and with bone
anger, shouted: Strike the rock!
No witnesses now, or ever!
We must have water.

Not as you heard.
The rock was dry. We were to die,
here: our ivory white bones,
last bond, bare to the sun

AFTER EDEN

We slept on the edge of town, in the last building
before desert. Freight trains carried salt
all night through our sleep, rusted boxcars
from forty years before clanging north, then south
at the edge of town. We could have forgotten
that wandering, but there were still dreams
of thirst and yellow winds.

By dark morning, our car parked in the last light
of the last streetlamp, our eyes narrowing,
we saw late the side window shattered
around a hole at the center: Cain's splintered
web across our foreheads in the glass.
We could have forgotten that mark, still
stunned to be so far from Eden.

GRAVEL TONES

We know only that he let go
of the rope and dove deeper.
His friends did not follow.

Panic emptied their tanks.
Now, black pearls
that were their eyes.

His father waits daily
at the sea's edge
for the body that will not

wash up. *Drown, bright alto
star: all cold and hunger
and claws. There is only*

*this dark tenor sea:
gravel tones, black kelp
constant longing.*

We too watch for boats,
like a lighthouse, stroke
after stroke: terrorist dinghy,

refugee raft - last human clutch
slipping. All sound, swollen.
And we are still startled

(Did he remember suddenly
white surfaces, and the smell
of air? Or by then,

a fish, last breath,
was he at peace
in a place with no sky?)

by the long winged shadows
crossing the sand long after
the dark gulls have gone.

RUTH BEKER

LORD OF THE BLUES

Oh God
lord of the blues
you knew all along
when you broke down

that garden wall
there would never
be enough love to go
around that evil

waits at every corner
and angels can never
be found when you need
them and that we cry

each night into our
prayer book knowing
the messiah won't
come while we're around

THE SEASON

I walk with my arms around
myself and try to spend the
aging day which above me
moves so gracefully and below
with me staggers fractured
and worn and me trying in
vain to patch it up and
thinking I cannot wear this
day again. Ever.

And yet in the morning I
pick it up again and put
it on me and we walk out
on the street my arms hugging
me tight and safe looking for
a way to spend time never
daring to look around and
see how nature so smoothly
minds its errant ways.

When I was younger the days
moved themselves. I never
had to urge them or think
up new things for them to
do. They knew and I sure
in their knowledge would
dance following close behind.

GAVRIEL BEN-EPHRAIM

WHERE ARE THEY, THE SCRUFFY BRILLIANT ANARCHISTS

I used to meet them, the scruffy brilliant anarchists
in the 60s, at the Queens College writer's workshop
or the "small caf" (the "big caf" was for fraternity jerks)
or in the Village, or at City College,
or at that trendy bar near Columbia,
I forget its name.
were they really smart or was I really dumb?
they'd read all of Blake
quoted long passages from *The Four Zoas*
wrote long poems that sounded like Blake
did spellbinding analyses of *Viridiana*
just like that
knew Indian mysticism
told touching stories about little Buddhist boys
wrote papers about Stalin and Mao
quoting in Chinese and Russian
married black girls
disappeared into San Francisco
left college without taking a degree
lived in lofts, played the piano like Lennie Tristano
played the drums, each in a different rhythm
harvested tobacco in Cuba
died obscurely
smiled embarrassed when I mentioned Israel
got A+ on college papers and didn't care
had long hair in 1964
peed over the palisades
had girlfriends who peed over the palisades
played guitar like Woody Guthrie
twanged the banjo or ukulele
strange old West Virginia tunes
had mothers in the Communist Party
worked part-time off-off Broadway
where are they?
they didn't become academics
I know all the academics
and they're not them
didn't become artists because they weren't artful
I think they're all dead now
Or maybe we are.

16

EUGENE DUBNOV

AND IN THE SUMMER

And in the summer
The soft grass in your garden,
With its bench,
Its view over the city lights below,
And the shrubbery near the fence
Where once I kissed a girl;
And the light
Shining on the white table in the porch
When the garden was dark,
In the very heart of the city,
The flowers which remained open at night,
And the house,
Your husband's photograph on the side-board,
And your daughters,
Your grandchildren
Playing tennis on the lawn.

And now the house and the garden are sold.
The summer is over.
Here the trees are swept by the wind,
The wind which sways the large grasses
And throws deep unquiet shadows.
The wings of the flowers are falling,
And the long and narrow leaves are wet.
The perishing of the branches is near.

EDWARD CODISH

from THE VOYAGE TO GAZA

13.

My friends have all been nomads like myself
wandering seas and lands and twisting *wadis*
across and through the homes and habitations
of Abels, settled Saxons, *fellahin*,
looting their hearts and money, taking wives
and leaving fast before the lure of place
unplundered, peaceful, full of changes all
revolving with the sun and coming back
ever to harvest, and to undried meat,
fresh bread, and aged wine, could tempt them from
the joys of ravaging fame and making names
which spread yet farther than themselves
and set their bodies, more than their victim's farms
ablaze. All these have died, or wandered on.

THE MIDDLE AGES

His sword wasn't, exactly, rusty,
more unpolished, dull, except the blade
and point. An excellent weapon still,
the lack of glitter arguing hard use
without time off for cleaning. When it whirred
over his head, the sun skittered only
at the sharpness, outlined the purpose,
the spirit of the thing. Body was just there
to hold the edge. In his old age, his arms
tired, his will to slash patterns in the air
gone, he'll make it gleam, burnish the steel,
I think he'll plate the hilt, engrave his name
along the gutter where blood ran. Then
maybe, he'll die and then, perhaps, it will rust.

THERE IS A WHITE BUTTERFLY

Despair was listening to baseball on the radio,
picking the phone up and not using it,
sleeping till noon on workdays, throwing
the mail away unread. I miss all that.

Now, despair is drinking myself to sleep
or hate, at day's end, waking at 3 AM
and no late movie, soon, nothing to eat.
The mailman hasn't been around in weeks.

There is a white butterfly on the marigold
and no one to show it to. Maybe brain cancer
would get me out of this, or you will,
or some other masturbatory fantasy.

I look at the white butterfly on the marigold
its black mouth buried in that tangerine;
the blue veined wings, unsynchronized, are wavering,
the compound eyes see everything, except ahead.

ELAZAR

COCKROACH

Look at the ugly cockroach if you can?
Except for the mind,
it is in every way superior to man.
See how it clings to the crumb
hides in dark places pretending to be dumb
always near water, underground
through pipes and old plumbing crawls,
can walk upsidedown on ceilings and walls
hatching broods racially perfect and profound.
How many generations have little whiskers
(antennae quavering at the prospect
of food) quavered, perched upon feces,
slime discarded and slop personified?
Yet older than man this little creature of God
defies extinction, ever tenacious
in its disgusting immortality.

A HORSE

I would be a horse, yes sir, if I could one day
amount to something, I would try to be a horse
even for a little while, just to see what it feels like
inside, and to sleep standing up. Yes sir,
a thorough-bred horse on a stud farm
to get a massive erection and mount a mare
and to plunge it into horse ecstasy, horse flesh
and all into virgin horse cunt, probosciously, and to have horse sex
and eat hay and sugar cube and salt-lick
and to make massive horseshit on wide open fields
for mushrooms to grow-
and my tail, and my mane, and my beautiful horse's balls

LEAF INSECT

To be eating leaves all day, my God
to be a leaf insect from Sri Lanka
to look so much like a leaf yourself and to be surrounded
by such an inexhaustible supply of green leaves
to eat, never to go hungry
until my God, one day another leaf insect comes along
and mistakes you for a leaf.

THE ELEPHANT

This is my world
it was made just for me,
it belongs to me,
it runs perfectly
like a little elephant
that glows in the dark.
It's completely predictable,
it was perfect when I found it,
but then I dropped it by mistake
Ho hum, it's just a world
I never thought it would break.

So my life has a life of its own
so it combs its hair
but it's not my head's hair upon,
it laughs when I cry
it cries when I laugh,
when I see an elephant
it sees a giraffe!
Ho hum, my life has a life of its own,
It will be home when I am not home -
it might even answer the telephone.

ELEGY FOR HEISENBERG

Beyond innocence
is a world of Heisenberg's
'uncertainty principle"
if it will A or B
or curve into C
and in what Frequency
these Quantum Mechanics
of the love
between (molecules) of you and me.
It's enough that light is
absolute / time inconstant
It's enough to make a song to play yr flute

Science is pure poetry as the stars grow more distant
as we Hubble around the telescope
listening for the arrival of a beat
waiting for the rush of a wave
or wavelength of particle love.

ZYGMUNT FRANKEL

WAKING UP IN THE MORNING

Waking up in the morning
my unshaven cheek feels against the back of my hand
as if time, having eaten up another twenty-four of my hours,
left the crumbs on my face.

TEL AVIV

There are no cockrels crowing at dawn in Tel Aviv
(and if there were, they would believe it is their crowing
that makes the sun rise).

And no bells on the synagogues either;
we go to our weddings
to Mendelssohn's march, and to our graves
to the intonation of the Kaddish.

There are only alarm clocks,
ambulance and police sirens, drivers honking their horns,
and people calling each other idiots.

And, at night, the screeching of lovemaking cats;
(perhaps small loves, like those of cats, are loud,
and great ones, like mine for you, silent).

And afterwards an abandoned kitten,
wailing throughout the evening and the night,
finally giving out in the small hours.

There are no nightingales in Israel.

WITH ALL THE

With all the
pills
IUDs
condoms
safe periods
coitus interruptus
abortions
accidents
wars
and emigration

why is the bus so crowded?

WE ARE A NATION

We are a nation with bearded and lustful kings,
that lives between the stones of an old wall;
between floods and locusts.
(Trying to keep a little above the floods and below the locusts.)

God watches from above, and vultures from telegraph poles.

So many of our women are old maids and young war widows.

THE BLACK CAT

I was walking along a deserted street one evening,
and a black cat jumped off a garden wall
and crossed the street in front of me.

I smiled.

I made two parachute jumps on a single Friday,
and swam in choppy seas on a thirteenth,
and could walk without mishap under all sorts of ladders;
so I just chuckled after the black cat,
and walked on,
                on my way to the party
where I met you.

ADVENTURES

It's nice to remember adventures
long after they have happened
now that one knows that they have ended well:

one did not miss that charging lion;
one did not catch anything from that woman;
one did not rot in jail in that banana republic;
and none of the planes have crashed.

The outcome wasn't so sure while the adventures were happening;
one was either hot,
or thirsty,
or sick,
or drunk,
or dying,

or several or all of the above.

The adventures were raw material for memories at the time,
and something of a handicap ever since;
without them, one could have invented better ones

WILLIAM FREEDMAN

PARTS IN LOVE

There is a pain in my shoulder
that will not stay still.
When it diminishes
where I feel it most
it finds another home.
Perhaps without my noticing
my shoulder brushed a woman's on the train
and was lost forever.
Who is to say
parts of bodies cannot love?
Sauce for the heart,
they might have said as wisely,
is sauce for the pancreas or spine.
Nothing explains so well, I think,
why they call this pulsing
adaptation of peculiar parts,
this local meshing, "making love,"
even when all the rest are strangers.
I can feel my elbow
longing for yours.
I know what we will learn
more stupidly and slow
locked arm in arm.
I swallow hard as I say this,
wondering what sweetly curved
Modigliani throat
with knowledge hoarded to itself
has turned my way.

OCCUPIED TERRITORY

Who knows what moved here once,
a few hundred meters from the sea?
There is a house here now,
a balcony, furniture, and death.
All things that make a life.
But the sea once traveled here
and did not feel it was trespassing.
It had a right, and one fish
surprised another where I sit.
We are all ghosts,
sweeping through one another's flesh,

the space it held,
squatted in like a landlord
and left without notice.
There are streets in this world
where I alone am a demonstration,
a gamut population leaning home.
We imagine where we've been
feels nothing, does not groan
or break when driven through.
No space, unoccupied, remains.
Nothing can be done there,
without injury to the spirit, as they say,
not knowing whose.

AND WHAT

And what
if out of the soft grey sea
a wave rose up
higher than the moon
and hunched the moon inside it
like a lantern sheltered in a cape,
that those who see
will not be seen,
and then returned
with so little troubling of the surface
mothers did not call to children,

leaving the great white light
pressed between the layers of the sea
that is no reflection,
leaving all who, like the planets,
stare to wonder
how, if it has left the heavens,
it has kept its light

and remember how the sea
unchanged, rowed like memory
from the pale deferred insistence
of the lost.

ROBERT FRIEND

TWO NECKLACES

That necklace rusting in a drawer -
I bought it for her birthday
but could not bring myself
to give it.
Though I kept promising myself
some day I would,
I never did.
Years later,
fastening casually
a necklace round her neck,
the first one long forgotten,
my hands
surprising her
surprising myself more
gripped tightly
as if they meant to choke her
and pressed
and pressed.
She stood terribly still.
Did she know what they were strangling?
When their grip loosened,
I was married to myself forever.

FRED

Dying of the blood cancer
he had held off for years, he had one wish left:
to take a last dip in the sea
that washed his beloved Tantura.

And so, wearing his bathing suit,
bundled and gathered up
into his car,
he was driven by his wife
to the edge
of that longed-for water.

Too feeble to swim,
too feeble even
to take a step
into the water,

he sat on the sand
reaching
as far as his toes could stretch
into the waves.

The June sun poured its diamonds,
the little hill watched
over the reef-protected bay.
Cloudlessly
the sky stretched
to the end of the world.

ARABIC LESSON

for Joyce

"Ahel", Arabic for "family",
cognate of "ohel", the Hebrew word for "tent" -
for desert dwellers a home:
grandfather, grandmother, father, mother, kids -
a family,
all under one roof -
their floor sand
covered by mats,
their roof and walls skin
flapping in the wind.

A Bedouin living in our kind of house
solid against the weather
complains,
"I can't sleep. The walls don't move."

SHALOM FREEDMAN

WITH AGE THE COSMOS IS SMALLER

With age the cosmos is smaller,
The rules of civilization's rise and fall
contract to minor questions,
Great issues of the day become
newspaper debates for strangers.
The conquering of the world
is a task for ignorant youths and middle-aged fools,
All great movements in time
sweeps of generations and decades
become history's nonsense song.
        With age the cosmos is smaller
        and the minor wounds
        of our own cursed and cankering bodies
        become the alpha and omega
        of Mind.
                Our minor minds, our own little human universes
                become the galaxies themselves
                vaster than all the stretches of stars
                there have been or ever will be.
                    In the end
                    we are the few people
                    we love,
                    and a dark space which is waiting somewhere
                                    in the night for us
                    and a cry to God for the white light in the distance
                    in which we are picked up like a baby,
                    and taken home to our mother
                    at last.

28

ALOMA HALTER

VOYAGE

When I try now to recall how the waiting was then I see us
tied to individual masts of time and space
yet floating on the sea of our letters.
The waves - the envelopes - rippled out with searching love
which the faint tune of our thoughts
carried across distant tides.

THE VOYAGE IS OVER

Then, through countless nautical miles
you trawled me in your thoughts
But now, the voyage over,
my time has lapsed: yesterday
last month. One year.
The harbour is out of sight.

Yet wasn't it, wasn't it different?
Moments that had always been
moored outside time,
like a breath held at the back of the mind.
Memories sheltered from the trade-winds
of everyday life.

GERSHOM GORENBERG

THE LEXICON OF LONGING

Section VI

halfcaste *v.* "Half magic, half reckless driving," Joe said,
"I mean, what man doesn't believe she's a demiwitch,
and that if he stirs his stinking drop
in her hot cauldron
he'll make himself again, or make the hero
he should have been?"

isochronal *adj.* In the philosophy of Ibn Barniya,
refugee and atheist, who changed his name to Ibbenburen
before leaping from the roof of an immigrant hostel
in Hamburg, the unmarked line that crosses a series of lives
at the same point, say when they met Susan
or when she left them, or the first night that Galyah, Melanie
or my daughter slept with a man
whose last name she didn't know,
or the hour, painted in black and red,
when a careening truck or bomb next to the bank entrance
shredded the babysitter, remember dear, with blue eyes
(which may also be the line marking
when God went missing) - these, wrote Ibn Barniya,
mark the only map worth needing - or the day
you noticed age was carrying you away
from your home country not toward it
or when you read on page 18 of the paper
that one more refugee had died on a street in Hamburg.

journeyman *n.* 1. Ulysseus, Iskander, Sinbad,
Avraham al-Batiti, a slippermaker of Sicily,
who according to a twelfth-century papyrus found
in a synagogue in Fustat, sailed from Sudan
to Ceylon, returning with sixty bales of cinnamon
(*ah-hai,* said a stevedore, *the stink of Eden and riches*),
and he now the color of cloves
and who despite sons, wives, and courtyards could not plant himself
but sailed again, blaming his "traitor soul and her whisperings"
of beasts, truth, and unending seas.
2. At sixteen, he ached against sidewalks like chains,
pored over roadmaps like scripture,
tried Trotsky, sex in the ass, fasting and Buddha
and got nabbed in mid-sky by a stewardess
after he strolled onboard the sixthirty three-stop to Sri Lanka.

Watch him now, enmortaged, enwifed, on the night shift
scrolling through Asian datelines on Reuter,
are there gales blasting at the backs of his eyes?

kurrajong *n.* A flavor of evening, like allspice,
when the boy wraps himself in your lap
and sleeps to the beat of your reading -
the curve of his back is a psalm,
the curve of his back balks account -
bitter now, bitter, like a mouthful of allspice, like ash,
when you remember the jeep that caught Haim's boy
on the border road (training accident, said the captain)
and cracked him, and how does Haim live now
with the kurrajong taste of his nights?

lepidosiren *n.* Not her hair, a black sea,
not her gold sax that sang dreams,
not the way she wavered between tables
as smoke would, wisp of waist, cloud
of breasts, nor the scent
of her cinnamon skin, but that language
he didn't know, stolen from fire,
or gods, or deserts unmapped, that unwritable sigh
to a man who had written wars and widowhood
on deadline every night for 32 years, made Joe untie himself from the
and cross an ocean to the address   [mast
that she gave him and never had lived at.

SHIRLEY KAUFMAN

"THE WEST IS SUFFERING FROM COMPASSION FATIGUE"

Mornings they rake the paths at the villa,
trim the boxwood. clear the dead pansies.

The mountains are blue all day, a cool
unflappable hush over the lake.

Before lunch we take turns with
the Herald Tribune. And over the pasta

we talk about change. Evenings we gather
in the grand salon sipping Campari

or the clear licorice of Sambuca,
coffee beans floating on top.

How courteous we are. Musical voices
and phrase-book Italian and optional

lectures. Afghanistan or fish.
Slides of the swamp eel in India

slithering. Ancient air-breathing mutants
that drown in water. I think of them

gasping in the mud when the rivers dried,
glassy fish eyes exploding out of

their sockets, the ones who made it, lungs
unfolding, spongy, one lobe at a time.

Some days we walk in circles
in a thin rain, connecting dots

in a child's puzzle, tiny blisters
of light on the wet topiary,

unnatural forms that crouch there
blinking. Some days I write poems

in the classic arbors, eased by the symmetry
of terraced gardens, the slow diligence

of natural selection. Click of the shears
as they whittle the hedges into peacocks.

THE LAWNS OF DELHI

On the lawns of the Mogul Gardens,
on the lawns of the International Center,
on the freshly mowed grass of all
the roundabouts in Delhi,

women squat in their saris
pulling up weeds.
They loosen their roots with their bony
fingers, pluck them out whole.

The women crawling on their cropped green
are small and bent. They squat
in the heat in their bright saris.
Their hands are dry twigs.

There is no shade but the shadow
of their bodies. How quiet
they are. Late in the morning
when the sun's in our eyes,

they become invisible.

FOR DEAR LIFE

It is the month before the leaves
fall, everything hanging on
for dear life. When I stop
on the path where lizards run
in and out of the borders, one
lizard stops with me. It chased
its shadow up the steep side
of the hill. Now it stands still
and together we study a marigold
next to the ivy. We both breathe
as softly as we can to keep it
from moving, to keep this minute
from slipping into the next.

SHARON KESSLER

MATERNITY HOSPITAL

for Rivanna

In the maternity hospital
new mothers wheel their infants
down the corridor
in carts like the ones
at the mini-mart.
Their babies peer out
trusting as cabbages.

Through the glass door down the hall
a row of babies wails;
each spotty face
wrinkles like a bruised peach.

At the nurses' station I overhear
one say to another:
It's time for that woman in 234
to check out
and I can't wake her.
Her husband is downstairs,
the baby is ready,
she has three others
waiting at home,
and she just goes on sleeping.

NIGHTWATCH
for Noga

At night,
in the hours
of no motherwarmth,
I stumble
towards the whimpering
that rises
out of the dark.
Go back to sleep, I hiss,
but mother-rage
is better comfort
than being left alone.

34

Mommy, sit here.
So I sit beside her,
breathing her back
into the furry skin
of a dream.
An hour later
the darkness
bursts forth in another song.
I rise to it.
She can't say what fear
stirs her, what cry
rings out unanswered in her sleep.
I've told her nothing
of the lives she has escaped from,
yet something
in her knows, and so,
I take her back
to lie beside me,
rescue her
from what I can.

JEAN KADMON

FREE WHEELING

after careful observation
I have decided
the birds can
keep their wings because
a bicycle likewise whizzes
and when tired
I've a more comfortable rest
than on a wire.

also - birds have no hands
to reach out.

this morning, however, although
from the ridge above the Kidron
I did have satisfactory view
of domes, towers, and early light,
my hands on the handle bars
could not reach you.

about bicycles and birds, therefore,
my judgment rests.

OLGA KIRSCH

AT THE CAGE OF THE BENGAL TIGER

> Leo tigris, great cat of Asia, is the largest member of the cat
> family. Only the lion can equal it in strength and ferocity.
> It can be dangerous to man. It lives in forests and swampy
> areas and hunts by night.

But here, passes its days
pacing the perimeter
of a narrow triangle
of caged space
whose apex is the rock
where its mate
dangling like an empty coat
drowses through the hours.
Treads, treads
tail a taut switch
haunch shoving
skull bumping
the bars.
Orange rage, ferocious flame
smoky with desperation.
The raggedest sparrow
scavenging in the dust
is luckier,
flits between the bars
goes anywhere it wants.

CHARLES KORMOS

CONVERSATION

We exchanged poems.
She gave me Shakespeare's.
I gave her mine.

She misunderstood
what I said.
I understood
what she didn't say.

MISPRINT

Instead of reading
what was there
I saw
what should have been
and blamed myself
for the mistake
others made.

MOST

Angry old men
are angry because
they never had
or no longer have,
or never knew
what they wanted most.

ORIT KRUGLANSKI

I RECALL

Only the ocean lies between us,
and all its silent life.
relax into fond remembering:
love,
like a squid in a bubble bath,
caught me by surprise.

UNTITLED

Of all the opportunities I've missed
I miss the most the possibility of dance
powerful imitations of softness and pink
steel bodies aching with pain
human hearts aching with pain
at their early deaths
buried in small studios
surrounded, perhaps, by six year olds
like my sister,
and me - clumsy,
forever in the beginners' class
I could have danced for joy
when she said
"Ballet is boring
I'm not going anymore"

LAMI

DRINKING FROM THE CROOKED CUP

I take it from the display on the shelf
Trace its distortions, encompassing its misfortune
With a rather stubby finger.
It is as grey as the clay it comes from
It is the color of my drooping blouse
And the vibrant unruly strands
After the pedantic haircut which didn't succeed.
The coffee is strong and does not dribble
The cup has weight and a bit of history.
In her last years, her gyrations were all off.
A crude potter's wheel, often flamboyant
At the wrong speed.
Crude   says cruel   to me
As I drink from her crazed cup
The one at the end of the row.

RED PECAN DUST; A SMALL WINNER

At rest from the closures of
Unread books
Skirting the weed-fringe in the
Violet patch
Setting handfuls of nuts
On the checkered table; they are
Markers
For the hidden verbs
For the exclaimed
Remarks
Preferred in the
Sounds a nutcracker
Musters
Cracking at the shells
With no remorse
With no infidelity
Alone with their sentences
Small industry for one.
Rusty dust
Good hours as the sun cools shadows
Pecan in curled hands
Wanting the smoothness of marbles
Betting, bettering one's self
At the shell-game
Small prizes
Always won
By others.

MARK L. LEVINSON

ON BEING MISIDENTIFIED
AS A DOCTOR OF LITERATURE

No, I'm a patient of literature.
A long library table makes me want
to stretch out trustingly and warm my socks
like soft bookends under the low lampshade;
for I'm impatient of literature,
won't read what won't fit into my back pocket.
Unholstering a book like a hipflask,
I post my finger at the chapter's end
to mark the dose I'll take; then pass it by.
Descriptions are forgotten; characters
are all filled in for by my relatives,
workmates, anyone whose name the author
echoes. His words in turn oint them over
in a complacent obliterature.

THE SUPERMARKET
(a study in senility)

At this aisle a staffer offers capsules
beside a free-standing cardboard gene clef,
and the shelves stock, in ascending order,
Eggplant, Gazpacho, Beans, Demerol, Fudge.
I speak of notes lined up on chromosomes:
dominant, subdominant, recessive.
I pluck from them my choice of sharps and flats
as down the aisle I wheel my sharping cot.
Only my feet are dreaming; they are warm
while my cheeks, tight with air conditioning
and with suspicion, smile at the cashier.
These feet are far from supermarket tiles.
They dwell with things safely paid for, and they
speak of the softness of going to bed.

TOURISTS

Glance upward from a life of trying not
to be a tourist: there they are, walking
Jerusalem's walls; ants on dead breadcrust.
They walked the wall of China and turned the
Chinese into China watcher watchers.
In Egypt they are shot, from time to time.
I too would rather not explain myself,
not make public all but the unexplained,
not retreat to the kids' room as the guests'
suitcases flagstone the parental floor.
Not be the contemplative foretopman
who wonders whether to alert the crew,
but be the ape who hears his own watchcry
before he knows he's seen the lion move.

SIMON LICHMAN

LIBERTY PEELING IN THE SUN

from a Pilgrim's journal

"Years on. How many saw the yachting on the Hudson? How many carved so deep that what remained was space into which we dreamed we'd pour our souls. We fled on boats called 'The Mayflower' and 'The Glory', 'The Golden Ladies' and 'The Arm of Liberty' - i.e. 'what crimes' *(what crimes?)* 'committed' *(what were their names?)*"

1.

Light between the rafters and the rails.
No hint of flower
whistles through this dug-out rock.
The arm waves full of hollow sunlight
(From France, they came, 'Join us'.)

2.

Sweet corn sunk through fishponds
rotted cars and cable reels.
Besuited men beside their polished steel
spade-to-hands beneath an open sky.

3.

I'd never seen those New York days.
The misbegotten
eye their wait into my nights.
*(I must not sleep
if the shoes fit and they're mine.)*
Manhattan. Wharves.
(Keep candles bright.)
Not brave. Nor indigo.
Call the ships to harbour.

Desert for gold.

THE BEAR BEHIND

There are night songs in the air that will not fade.
Car doors connect, motors whine, walls hum.
I listen for the quiet sounds
of sleepers in their midnight chests
tinkerbells and crocodiles
of hedgehogs browsing in the garden
and fieldmice scavenging rabbit food.
These are the tunes that turn this waiting round.
Put back the essays on their shelf.
Stack the children's books.
Arrange the small blue vase on the old mahogany desk.
Take out my bears and racing cars.
Watch the night unfold behind the morning star.
Let my shadow slide across this page.

WAITING FOR SLEEP: NETANYA
20 / 12 / 91

Listening to the sound of sea and cars
coming off the coastal plain
writing notes to myself
on your familiar scraps of paper
to be there in the morning
should sleep come.
How the moon can close in on winter nights
to chill the heart -
but always there was light and laughter
with you leading us towards
the first bluebells of Ashridge
moorhens by the broken bridge of Aldenham
singing through the red and blue book
sleepy journeys home.

FAY LIPSHITZ

SUMMER

Two tiny, delicate insects
Hold sexual congress
On the rim of my water glass.
Her bright body
Flat against the edge.
He, glued to her centre,
Tilts skywards.
They are beautiful. Tiny black heads
Interrupted by a flash of silver.
No, the black is all blank eye,
The head silver. Sheer wings
drop glittering sideways.
He ripples with tiny movements,
His body growing thinner.
But now his rocking
Brings them to the edge. They tilt
Over, slide
Towards a sea below.
But wait.
A gathering of strength,
They cling
To sheer glass, haul
Crawl, and gain the top, still locked.
And rest. We look away
An instant then turn back.
They're gone.
Two gleaming scraps, torn, tossed apart,
Frantic in the water.
You leap up, race with glass aloft
Past wondering faces
Dash lovers, water, out across the grass.
To seek, to find, not find,
Increase, die.

ROCHELLE MASS

LIKE A COMPASS BOUND FOR NORTH

Some men walk with thick thighs
and flat feet
growl commands
take only what they want with yellowed hands
with dull eyes they stare down their prey.

Some men walk with soft steps
meeting lovers on the way
offering warmth like a compass
bound for North

They stroke a woman's neck
shaking doubts from her lips
placing jewels on her eyes.

JOANNA MORRIS

TELL ME

Tell me it's not true
as you slip your arm over her shoulder.
tell me it never happened
though the smell lingers on your fingertips.
tell me you didn't do it
as I lie in bed, listening to the radio,
writing letters

JESUS

late last night,
in the middle of town,
i saw jesus
riding side-saddle
on a motorbike.
of course, i
recognized him
by the blond
hair and leather
sandals. i know
jesus when
i see one.

REENA RIBALOW

MEMO TO MYSELF

Note the phases of your face.
You are near completion,
drawing full your tides
to shore.
Just that flooded hour.
You will lose the swell
and dwindle now,
diminished,
patient,
pregnant
as the moon.

LONG DISTANCE IN THE LAUNDROMAT

The air is savory with laundries;
leaning on an impotent machine,
I cry,
blurry and unfocussed
as a washer's eye.
Intravenous consolation
trickles through
the detumescent wire.

I am adrift on disinfected seas;
simply for this minute,
I decode
the message of a thousand
agitated loads.

AIR PERSISTS

Ah, your cupped palms;
I lie so small within.
My pale asphyxiated flesh
feeds the lust
of your solicitude.

Your love
eliminates the need for salt.

RIVA RUBIN

THE KEEPER IS WILD

In Sarajevo the zoo is under gunfire.
An anguished keeper gauntly dodges
mortars on dappled lawns
and climbs cagewire to fling
clumps of grass to carnivores -
lions like floormops fall against the bars,
a tiger near a tiger lies rotting under flies
and the bear makes a kiss-mouth for tiny apples.

INNOCENCE

The pretty monkeys in the park
nibbled pilfered icecream cones.

(I thought the Hindus such hypocrites,
waving their woven banana leaves,
pretending not to protect
the piled fruit on their stalls.)

A big one dropped from a branch and snatched
the icecream cone from my hand.
I stamped my foot and he made me see
the furious god in his eyes.

My mother, not knowing, hit him
with her sunhat.

SNAKEMOUTH

Into your snake laugh, whose rush
I hear only by silent and fastidious listening,
I slide
Past the stony rim of your lips
you hiss me in, to your snake warmth
fanged and safe

SOUND OF FIRE

I've heard about a sound iron sings out of rocks.
Between us is a bronze sea
greening and flaking on my lips.
My tongue
has burst against fire.
My hand, my son, lies mute in your hair.

DIALOGUE

Beginning
its dissolution the Soul enters
a diseased state: it takes on
human form. (Cebes to Socrates)

It would be better

to clench into a star-shaped nodule
grey and dry
like spiders that die
fisting around themselves
under the oleander.
Or to sit motionless like monkeys
in a pocket of deadly liana
contemplating the cages
stacked inside them.
Or to weep dry ice and mourning
fill moonflowers with blindness
or to tilt on ledges
with hinged wings
like closed leather umbrellas
and a barbedwire grin on face with no cheeks
only eyes like toadstools.

In dead silence

something cartwheels into the mist
vanishes while the smells of worship
and lovemaking - sandalwood, tapersmoke
and candlewax melting - fold in from the sea

SHIMON PALMER

UNTITLED

i am like some small measly creature
scurrying around and waging silly little wars
thrashing through mangled flesh, wallowing in the gore

to paddle back to you
a bloody strip of salvaged decaying meat dangling from my
                              clamped vulture's beak
for you.

HOLE

I roll on forever
non-absorbent
never know where I'm going
or where the fuck I've been.

A crater suddenly looms
in the vast typhoon of advance,
breach created
yawning deep within me -

I feel your loss,
you are missing in my life.

RAQUEL SANCHEZ

PASSAGE I

I smell this language through your glass of dark cognac
    at the Everycorner cafe
    and sit with you to drink its translation
    unaccustomed

I'm caught between shesh-besh*
    and its voice in the colloquial humidity
    while you bang dice of better luck

We arrange ourselves to meet passers-by through hastened glances
and I try not to notice the me who is pretending not to notice you

All you men are the same
You're tightly held by fists of indecision

My hands open
    see the impression made by keys
    hang between hope / fear fingers
        along with a travellers prayer

How do I disintegrate to New York precautions
    which still make me
    and figure I'm the only one worthy of what's left
        as we ride our time in this far away city
            of benevolent concrete blankets

But ghetto images call me to
    war
        and conversations
            as the Tel Aviv soldiers glance back

I'm running out of patience for the page I want to be
    and quietly
    however watching
        the excitement of my innocence
I see I'm burning myself

*shesh-besh: Backgammon

REVA SHARON

from AWAITING GENESIS

Each year he had to poll his hair
it grew so heavy on his head
And when the burden of his curls
was weighed in the balance
in exile in Geshur at home in Jerusalem
he took no account of the scales
for he recognized

the color and fire as his sister's
before she dressed her hair with ashes
and rent her robe of many colors -
Long nights he heard her crying
and then her silence
in the cool dark of her room .
which their father never entered

———

If what endures is stone
she is wedged in the strata of Judea

If what endures is word
she is a litany humming in our blood

If what endures is memory
recall her song from the stone

If what endures is clay
she was fired by an ancient sun

If what endures is vessel
lift her carefully from the rubble

If what endures is water
she flows from the Gihon Spring

If what endures is hope
breathe life into Tamar's name

GREEN CALLINGS

"The flowers appear on the earth;
The time of singing is come..."
                    Song of Songs II:12

Frogs sing
across the old walk
green mating songs
under a new moon

Moss has settled
between the bricks
we walked on   once
Tonight no light falls

on the path I walk
alone   between green callings
Tender grass sways in the fields
and the river is rising

Tomorrow will you take me
through the west hills
where I have never been
Will you let me

take you   barefooted
through the sands that claim me
Tomorrow will you call my name
Will I sing   for you

RICHARD E. SHERWIN

STONEHOUSE # 37

Twenty odd years I've lived in the gum grove
Wars, droughts, and governments have come and gone

Boiled my tea, warmed my balls, the one same stove
Leaves that were my shade, now my scent

Sitting on logs and listening to wind
Watching ants my mind gone vagabond

I think I've forgotten what talking meant
Rain cleans everything even sins

From NOMAD IN GOD

These furnaces are cold, my Lord, but colder
still the heart I offer you. The soul's
gone off with yours and's not been heard of since.
I's not as if they've left a word to mince.
Even holiness is rumored dust.
The Bible's language lost and silenced trust.
My enemies turn friends, my friends turn foes.
Salvation melts my mind like sun the snow.

Warm and happy snuggling into death,
the only happy ending I've not read
I whistle through the holes inside my head,
cooling graveyards down with saved-up breath.
Burning savorless I offer you,
my Lord, my self, my timeless barbecue.

TURNPIKE TRIUMPH

Forty-four years since
we rammed the Jersey Turnpike
through all night rain the
music breaking ears like dawn
our orange clouded eyes and

minds so sleepless.thick
the wipers windowed nothing
at all, ever since
you died on me, been driving
eighty with none to speak of

visibility
jalopy rattling wired on guts

56

faith blind luck you name
it trying to hold on what
cant be kept out, my eyes froze

open seeing more
than they want and not what they
look for tolls all paid
crashing barriers to sleep
waking so triumphant then

AUTUMN TANKA

I confront the wind
autumnally, the tree tops
rustling their applause.
We declaim each others fall.
Barely apprehending breath.

Written in one, read
in another, spoke in
a third wrong language,
our lives, untranslatable,
all, and yet I... and yet you...

Synagogues of palms
shivering hosannas, bare
the summer mind, sins
all harvested and offered
up atonement tithes, what psalms!

The first green citrons
in the shops, what promises
of sun distilling
oranges to warm us through
rains we're ready to pray for.

Wound up tighter than
a drum, as if the muggy
summer overturned
the keys, my mind wont rest till
stormclouds rumble loose the rain.

'Emptiness accepts
everything'. This raindrop now
splashing into mind.
These strings of water lashing
flesh. This storm drilling the earth.

NORMAN SIMMS

ENVIOUS OF A HERO

As when Odysseus that wily man, whose thoughts
were spoken in his guts, rolled around a problem
sausage-like upon the grating fire of his soul,
and listened to the barking of his heart,
so I come to this place today, this cold empty room
alone, unable to start a fire, and growl
over unruly feelings that whine at me
in half-articulate complaints. Who stole
the furniture, the tables and the lamps,
the bookshelves and my massive notes,
the heavy leather seat upon which my thoughts
rested and grew deep in voice? Where
are the salted peanuts I used to nibble,
the thick black beer, the Muses' service?
Voices in another room screech at me,
as when Athena flew to the roofbeams,
a swallow, wailing with the deathly pitch
of Pan's abortion-causing voice.
I try to write them down,
put them in a place, but my fingers
will not move in the cold, my ink is ice.
How can Odysseus that big man roll
his thoughts like sausages, and I
sit immobile, knotted in my guts afraid
of voices beyond the space of thought?
What bitch snarls at me and will not
let me lift her puppies, my faithful brood?
The gods no longer intervene.
They shriek out of doors.
The great tomes of wisdom now are tombs,
my study turned into a kennel for wild dogs.
Let this poem burst apart
and fill my world with words I have created,
and let the least, last spark glow!

ELAINE M. SOLOWEY

ENCOUNTER

Gazelles
In the scant shade
Poised
Amber-eyed

Horns polished
And curving
They feed
On the thorns

Lift heads
At my slow tread
In stillness
Appraise
And whirl
Gilt and iron
Their hoofbeats
Like rain

On the stones
Of the canyon
Where rain
Never falls.

ON WAKING

The dawn light
On the desert
A bird call
Dry, hot wind
Brown and tired
Without beauty
To the stranger
But to me
What I want to see
On waking
A lover's face
Grown old.

LOIS UNGAR

IS IT 1963 AGAIN

Is it 1963 again
and you and I young walking down the street
reciting poems to the wind
I've walked down this street with all the men I've loved
walked down this street
I don't remember words
I remember silence
and now you are filling me
with words of 1963
and I must decide if I want to listen

WIVES LIKE SAILORS

Her husband asked her if
she was getting ready for the great fuck in the sky
when she became affectionate
is that how he sees her
is she only loving when she makes love
She thought it was okay to be like that
hard like a sailor in port
to turn over and go to sleep afterwards.

ARTIE WALDORF

I was 9 when Artie Waldorf got out of prison
and grabbed my mother and kissed her
I know he just got out because
my sister stayed up late and listened
That winter his wife Frances wore lots of jewelry and mink coats
his son Jacky gave me my first kiss
Once he put his fist through my
mothers dumbwaiter when my uncle
Sammy's friend Cream Cheese
came on to Frances
It was the winter Frances wore all the jewelry and mink coats
or maybe it was the next one
that Artie got shot to death in a barbershop chair
Daddy said he probably wanted too much.

TO AMERICA

My husband has gone to America to get rich
while we decide what to do with the rest of our lives
on the way to the wedding we will stop in Paris
Anyone has only to read the sweetness of our poems to know
we lived right
But it looks as if the defeated us
I thought you could make a living
    growing strawberries
        or
    snowpeas
        or
    poems.

I REMEMBER THEM ALL AT THE AIRPORT

I remember them all at the airport
with their goodbyes and their hellos,
why do i wake up and think of you?
you're nothing to me -
you came through my life like a whirlwind.
i did better than jesus christ,
he only walked on the kinneret
i walked across the atlantic.
the tile floors are cold in september
the eastern sky is different than the west
the stars are upside down.

IT SLIPPED THROUGH MY HANDS LIKE WATER

It slipped through my hands like water
and i miss it
but it wasn't mine to have slipped so easily.
everyones demons are important to them
another mistake - demon
ouch again
was it a mistake - demon
or was it my soul
walking freely
and unavoidably
colliding with another soul.

CHAYYM ZELDIS

I MET THE CHILDREN

I met the children
on moonlit
snow:
- where do you go
at night -
I cried:
- so cold,
so blue,
you'll freeze,
the lot
of you -

they didn't answer.

- your mothers
will worry -
I said.

- no
our mothers are dead -

stricken
I told
my sympathy.

- keep still -
they sighed:
- so
are we -

SILENCE

Silence is
a
garden

Drifting
under
shapeless
moons

Waxed
with the
light of
brimming
stars

Silence is
a
garden

Bordered
by
the dead.

LINDA ZISQUIT

TOWARD

Dishes shine, quilt fluffed,
flowers spring with new sun.
But morning comes to waiting,
midday lull, this rage
when no one will leave me
to rummage through drawers
for another promise.
And when darkening day comes to
streets and bends I am craning my neck
for a sign, a number, some trace
of you. At night I close the books,
pull myself in to a tight column
of hope, hands at my sides
or between my thighs for warmth,
on my belly crawling.

LIKE SPEECH

I've seen one lie unspoken
release the deadly pack.
Like a hornet splitting the nest
as others scatter, realign.
We lived so long inside the buzz
it nestled in our ears like speech,
its fragrant nectar rested in our
care like home. Cruel ecstasy:
to hide from ourselves, entwined.
To ask: which one did us in?

DISARMED

And when she woke
she understood she would go on
hiding her deceptions.
Even the man
would remain in the dark.
She knew it was not love
as he defined it.

nothing to leave a life for

only another point on her map
of blind spots.

Yet she would rather play out the plot.

It was no longer necessity or compulsion
to unravel the truth,
how or why it started
in the amphitheater,
how in her mouth the word
'beginning' formed
with her knowledge of his certain
response.

What interests her now is the context,
her life as the setting
for disaster.

In fact no explanation
no attempt to see his choice
centered
can undo the perversity
of her disguise.

The only hope
is her inability
to repress anything.

ROGER WHITE

TRAVELLING BACKWARD

You enter in silence. Sadly,
almost sullenly, we strip,
achieve the frenzied arrival
in Braille impressed on our damp
and trembling skin.
The bed rebukes us, creaking disapproval.
Clothed again, we drink tea.
For the first time since entering
you speak, your *How've you been?*
hurtling us from the glib city
to modest suburbs where love might make its home
under the green and tended trees.
We are like passengers perversely
riding backward on a swift train
who already know the disappointment
of the destination, have left
the orange peel to wilt,
trampled the timetable underfoot.
Speaking now, reversing our journey,
you become truly naked,
I truly aroused.
Is to tell, be listened to,
our greatest lust?
O darling, I see danger in our travels.
If you speak my name but once in tenderness
I shall die under the wheels.

CONTRIBUTORS:

Ada Aharoni was born in Cairo and has lived in Israel since 1951. She is the author of twenty-one books, including a collection of poems *From the Pyramids to Mount Carmel.* She has received several prizes and award, including the British Council Literary Award, and is the editor of the Hebrew literary magazine *Galim (Waves)* and the founder of International Friends of Literature. She teaches literature and sociology at the Haifa Technion.

Karen Alkalay-Gut was born in England, raised in the U.S.A., and came to Israel in 1972. She lectures in English literature at Tel Aviv University. She has published books of poetry, translations, and biography. Her latest collection of poems is *Harmonies / Disharmonies.* She is a founding member and the present Chair of the Israel Association of Writers in English.

Rachel Tzvia Back lives in Maoz Zion and teaches English Literature at the Hebrew University in Jerusalem. Her work has appeared in numerous journals including *The American Poetry Review, Sulfur, apex of the M* and *Ariel.* Her chapbook *Litany* was published by Meow Press in 1995 and additional work is forthcoming in the SUNY Press anthology *Dreaming the Actual: Israeli Women Writers in the 90s.*

Ruth Beker came to Israel from Seattle, Washington in 1961. She is a journalist and has published her poetry in the U.S.A. and Israel.

Gavriel Ben-Ephraim was born in Germany, raised and educated in the US, and came to Israel in 1970. He is a lecturer in English at Tel Aviv University.

Edward Codish lived in Israel from 1971 to 1987, and now teaches modern Jewish philosophy and English at Yeshivat Akiva in Lathrup Village, Michigan. He has recently published poems and essays on Judaism in the e-magazine *Ariga.*

Eugene Dubnov was born in Estonia and came to Israel in 1971. His work was published in the U.S.A., England, France, Canada, Australia, New Zealand, Germany, Russia, and Israel.

Elazar (Larry Freifeld) was born in the U.S.A. and came to Israel in 1982. He has published ten books, of which *A Jew in the House of Harvard* received the Israel Federation of Writers award in 1987. His most recent books are *The World According To Animals* and *Poet's Guide to the Holy Land.*

Zygmunt Frankel was born in Poland, grew up (deported) in Siberia, and lived in Belgium and England before settling in Israel in 1952. He has published novels, short stories, and poems in England, U.S.A., and Israel. His novel *Short War, Short Lives* was published by Abelard Schuman, and *Octopus* won the Adam International Review's short novel award. A collection of his short stories, *A Witch Growing Old,* in Hebrew translation, was published by Sifriat Poalim, and several of the stories were broadcast by the Israeli radio.

Shalom (Seymour) Freedman was born in the U.S.A. and came to Jerusalem in 1974. He writes on Jewish subjects.

William Freedman was born in the U.S.A., came to Israel in 1967, and teaches English Literature at Haifa University. His poems have appeared in many literary magazines, including *American Poetry Review, Literary Review, Antioch, The Quarterly, Iowa Review, Shenandoah* and *Dalhousie Review.*

Robert Friend was born in Brooklyn and has lived in Israel since the 1950s. He has published several books of poetry and translation, and lectured in English and American literature at the Hebrew University for over thirty years.

Gershom Gorenberg was born in the U.S.A. and came to Israel in 1977. His poems have appeared in English and American magazines, including *Argo,* the *Beloit Poetry Journal, California Quarterly,* and the *New York Quarterly.* He is a senior editor of *The Jerusalem Report.*

Aloma Halter was born in England and has lived in Israel since 1980. She is the assistant editor of *Ariel.* Her poems and translations have appeared in several magazines in Israel and abroad.

Jean Kadmon was born in the U.S.A., studied anthropology in Chicago, and settled in Israel in 1946. She is a visual artist as well as a poet. Her poems have appeared in various magazines and some of her work has been collected in *Clais and Clock* and in *Peering Out.* She also wrote *Moshav Segev,* an epic of the Six Day War.

Shirley Kaufman was born in the U.S.A. and has lived in Jerusalem since 1973. She has published seven collections of poetry in the U.S.A. and two books of translations, and received many awards and prizes. Her *Selected Poems* was translated into Hebrew by Aharon Shabtai and published by Bialik Press in 1995. Her latest book is *Roots in the Air: New and Selected Poems,* published by Copper Canyon Press in 1996.

Sharon Kessler was born in the U.S.A. and came to Israel in 1981. She lives in Pardess Hanna. Her publications include a collection of poems, *The Insistence of Names.*

Olga Kirsch came to Israel from South Africa in 1948. She writes in Afrikaans (7 volumes of poetry in South Africa) and English.

Charles Kormos, poet, journalist, and translator, was born in Romania and came to Israel after having lived in England. His latest collection of poems is *Star: At High Noon.*

Orit Kruglanski was born in Tel-Aviv and works as a script writer for interactive multimedia. She writes in English and Hebrew and translates between the two.

Lami (Halperin) was born in the U.S.A. and lives on a kibbutz. She writes in both English and Hebrew, and has published three collections of English poems: *Penumbra, Parlando Rubato* and *Durable Enscriptions,* and, in Hebrew, *Ad Gmar Ha Hatima.*

Mark L. Levinson was born in the U.S.A. and has lived in Israel since 1970. His work was published in Israel and the U.S.A.. He is currently the editor of the literary magazine *Voices Israel.*

Simon Lichman was born in London and has lived in Jerusalem since 1971. He lectures in folklore, literature and drama and directs the Traditional Creativity in the Schools Project. His published works include a book of poems, *Snatched Days.*

Fay Lipshitz was born in South Africa and immigrated to Israel in 1973. She lives in Jerusalem and works as a librarian. Her poems have been published in anthologies and literary journals in Israel and the U.S. She has also exhibited her drawings, etchings and monotypes.

Rochelle Mass was born in Canada, came to Israel in 1973, and lives in Jezreel Valley. She received several prizes and was short-listed in the 1991 BBC Radio Play Competition. She is also a painter and a sculptor, and has exhibited in Israel and Canada.

Joanna Morris was born in England and is presently working at the Jerusalem bureau of *Newsweek.*

Shimon Palmer was born in 1975 in Michigan and came to Israel in 1991. He is now serving in the army.

Reena Ribalow was born in the U.S.A. and lives in Jerusalem. Her work has been published in England, the U.S.A. and Israel and has won several literary prizes.

Riva Rubin was born in South Africa and came to Israel in 1963. Her publications, here and abroad, include five books of poetry, translations, and short stories, which have won several literary awards including the Dulzin Prize. She served on the Executive Board of the Israel Chapter of PEN for five years, and edited its 1993 English language anthology.

Raquel Sanchez, who was born in Paris to a Brooklyn mother and Venezuelan father, spent parts of her childhood in Spain, England, Venezuela and Morocco. She obtained her Master's degree in social work at Yeshiva University in New York, and worked in ghettos rehabilitating gang members and helping families in crisis. She came to Israel in 1994 and does similar work here.

Reva Sharon was born in the U.S.A. and has lived in Israel since 1987. Her published work includes a collection of poetry called *Pool of the Morning Wind*, and was the subject of a publication by Zurich University. She organises the Jerusalem AACI Series of Poetry Readings in English.

Richard E. Sherwin, born in the U.S.A., has lived in Israel since 1964. His poems have appeared in Israel, India, U.S.A., England, France, Australia, New Zealand, and Japan. *Nomad in God* is his most recent collection. He teaches English and American Literature at Bar Ilan University. His interests are the influences of Oriental Cultures on Western Literature.

Norman Simms was born and grew up in New York. After 25 years in New Zealand, where he had been active as a publisher, editor, reviewer, scholar, and writer, he settled in Israel in 1995 to teach at University of the Negev in Beersheva.

Elaine M. Solowey was born in the U.S.A., came to Israel in 1971, and lives on the kibbutz Ketura in the Negev, where she manages an experimental grove.

Lois Ungar was born in the U.S.A. and has lived in Israel since 1982. Her books of poetry, published in the U.S.A. and Israel, some in Hebrew translation, include *Miscarriage in Vermont, The Apple of His Eye, White Rain in Jerusalem , Poems Political* and *Tomorrow We Play Beersheva*.

Roger White, Canadian born, lived in Israel since 1971, in the service of the Baha'i World Centre in Haifa, and published three collections of poems and a novel. He died in 1993.

Chayym Zeldis was born in Buffalo and first came to Israel in 1948 where he worked on agricultural settlements and served in the army during the Sinai Campaign of 1956. He returned to the States on a creative writing scholarship in 1958, and settled in Israel again in 1989. He teaches at Tel Aviv University, and is the author of six novels and a collection of poetry. His poems in this book come from *Sparks (Gefen Publishers, Jerusalem)*.

Linda Zisquit was born in Buffalo and has lived in Jerusalem, teaching, translating, and writing poetry since 1978. Her work has appeared in journals in the U.S.A., England, and Israel. *Toward* is from *Ritual Bath (Broken Moon Press, Seattle, 1993)* and *Disarmed* and *Like Speech* are from *Unopened Letters (Sheep Meadow Press, N.Y., 1996)*.